A Kaleidoscope of Unfolding Womanhood

Tani O. Ifediora

BUDS, BLOSSOM, AND BLOOM: A KALEIDOSCOPE OF UNFOLDING
WOMANHOOD
by Tani Ifediora
Published by Creation House
A Charisma Media Company
600 Rinehart Road
Lake Mary, Florida 32746
www.charismamedia.com

This book or parts thereof may not be reproduced in any form, stored in a retrieval system, or transmitted in any form by any means—electronic, mechanical, photocopy, recording, or otherwise—without prior written permission of the publisher, except as provided by United States of America copyright law.

Unless otherwise noted, all Scripture quotations are from the King James Version of the Bible.

Scripture quotations marked AMP are from the Amplified Bible. Old Testament copyright © 1965, 1987 by the Zondervan Corporation. The Amplified New Testament copyright © 1954, 1958, 1987 by the Lockman Foundation. Used by permission.

Design Director: Bill Johnson
Cover design by Nancy Panaccione

Copyright © 2011 by Tani Ifediora
All rights reserved

Visit the author's website: www.courtoisieng.com

Library of Congress Cataloging-in-Publication Data: 2011942167
International Standard Book Number: 978-1-61638-744-0
E-book International Standard Book Number: 978-1-61638-745-7

While the author has made every effort to provide accurate telephone numbers and Internet addresses at the time of publication, neither the publisher nor the author assumes any responsibility for errors or for changes that occur after publication.

First edition

11 12 13 14 15 — 987654321
Printed in Canada

This book is dedicated to my precious daughters, young ladies growing still

Chioma Moyosore and Okwukwe Ifeolu-Mayokun

Contents

Author's Note ix
Introduction 1

Part I: Buds
Chapter 1: Birth 7
Chapter 2: Innocence 13
Chapter 3: Not So Innocent 19

Part II: Blossom
Chapter 4: Seasons of Change 29
Chapter 5: Crossing 35
Chapter 6: Celebrating Life 43

Part III: Bloom
Chapter 7: Petals 51
Chapter 8: Fragrance 55
Chapter 9: The Flower 59
Epilogue 63
About the Author 65
Contact the Author 67

Acknowledgments

I WISH TO EXPRESS my sincere appreciation to every single member of my lovely family: my sons of invaluable worth—Uchechukwu Olakunle, Chukwuemeka Oluponle, and Chukwuka Olurotimi—and my precious daughters, Chioma Moyosore and Okwukwe Ifeolu-Mayokun. Many times for the sake of this work I relegated them to second place in my timing schedule. Thank you for still opting to keep me as your mum! I love you dearly.

To my dear husband Chukie, an epitome of long-suffering in the course of the initial writings: thank you for enduring those many nights when I'd be so "inspired" I'd crawl out of bed to write entire chapters—only to scratch half my inspiration off under a second close and critical scrutiny. Your bed companion on such nights was your pillow.

I also wish to express my sincere gratitude to the many ladies whom I have come in contact with along life's journey. The avid interest you showed when listening to me and your voiced gratitude made me begin to realize that what I had to share was more valuable than I had realized.

To you, dear reader, who has chosen to read this book: thank you. I believe you won't be disappointed.

Finally, and most importantly, to the almighty God, my dear Father, who bestowed upon me the gift of writing; to my Lord Jesus Christ, the indisputable Word through whose light I pen my words; and to the Holy Spirit, whose touch of gentleness paints in vivid pictures the lines I jot forth, I say thank You, thank You, thank You!

In Jesus Christ, life truly is a fulfilling experience!

Author's Note

PAST DISCOURSES WITH young women brought to my realization the existing innuendo on subjects that I took for granted as normal and known. I never imagined I stood in the midst of a vat of ignorance but for the thirst with which a number of young ladies drank of my words.

This book is written with the simple aim of pointing the reader to a certain level of awareness. In touching on myriad areas of growth, I hope to give younger girls, as well as older women, the impetus and courage to broach intimate matters with each other. In presenting a kaleidoscope of my experiences and infusing into the story line the fictitious character named Flower, I hope to draw the reader into an intimacy that will give the subject being discussed a greater allure.

Overwhelmingly, the undertone of self-esteem and self-acceptance are recurring themes the length of this book. This conscious reminder of the need for a positive self-affirmation in the light of God's Word is necessitated primarily by the unimaginable number of bruised and hurting lives that surround us and with whom we daily are in contact.

Be blessed. My prayer is that the contents of this book, in an abundant flow of mirth and laughter, will bring knowledge to you, and in the wings of knowledge, the freedom of liberating truth.

Introduction

When God created man, He put everything He is into forming the crown of His creation. From the brazen handsomeness of man He brought out the delicate sculptured beauty of woman. Man was made in God's image. Mankind is the species (the kind), a group unique and not in comparison to any animal or bird. For although these also are creations (animals and birds), they are separate "kinds." It is therefore normal that mankind should be able to relate and communicate most effectively with his kindred (those of the same species as himself). It is an anomaly that man should experience conflict situations on the grounds of race and ethnic diversity.

In essence, mankind is composed of two genders: masculine and feminine. God informs us that from the onset He created man male and female. The story of Creation breaks down the course of events in a step-by-step description of how God knocked Adam down with a deep slumber and during the process of his sleep performed an incredible surgery on him by extracting from him a rib that He formed into woman.

Many tend not to realize that in this elaborate narration of man's creation, God is passing on an important message to all. In the man and the woman are the expressions of the character of God. In the masculinity and femininity are attributes of His Person revealed in the separate vessels of man and woman. Too many people erroneously push forward a portrait of a "macho" God. The world has tried to impress on people's minds a lopsided image of a "tough" God with an emphasis that man came in that unbalanced "God" image. The accurate depiction of a persevering, loving, and yet just God is seldom portrayed. What is portrayed is either an outrageous picture of a fearful, angry, and judgmental God or a distorted portrayal of a bashful Christ.

Now is the time for Christians to prove wise in throwing off the world's uninformed picture of our sovereign God and, based on this, rejecting its subsequent distorted image of man. It is crucial for man to know the purpose for his creation and what God's expectations for him are in behavior and living. The pages of the Bible reveal the exact representation of God in affections of sensitivity, compassion, kindness, and justice. Both male and female court those who produce like attention of caring and thoughtfulness. Such warmth is a human magnet drawing unto itself hurting humanity, famished for a taste of selfless love.

In today's fast-track world, womanhood has undergone a meteoric transformation. The mind assault is total in calculated and effectively mounted media hype. From billboards to television commercials, graffiti to music lyrics, the message is unfettered in direct insidious and ludicrous obscenities. Audio and visual debauchery are projected unrelentingly, a barrage blasted at the senses, an attack determined to guarantee a total mind decomposition.

For the young, values are confused. Wrong is presented as right, the macabre is made attractive, the gory turns routine, and insanity threatens to pervade erstwhile sanity. We live in times where deception is adorned in sophisticated coverings of seduction and allure. To counter the wild ravages of the world is the peaceful stability found only in the Word of God. The time is come to celebrate and exalt truth. The very preservation of our children's lives is fully dependent on the rock of truth, which alone is able to prevail against the chokes of secularism.

This writing is primarily for the woman, the sculpted beauty whose virtue is constantly under attack. I leave you with a final word to spur you on to a constant celebration of your uniqueness. Though the environment is set to sedate your senses, blunt your discernment, weather your speech into a colorless, conformist tone, and reduce your behavior to a hue of incoherent inconsistencies, you can and should remain your own unique person.

Your uniqueness is God's design. He created you for a specific purpose and will unfold the wraps of your destiny to you, as you yield to His will and lean on His grace.

I am living, breathing, proof positive of God's extravagant love.

Part I

Buds

Yea, the darkness hideth not from thee; but the night shineth as the day: the darkness and the light are both alike to thee. For thou hast possessed my reins: thou hast covered me in my mother's womb. I will praise thee; for I am fearfully and wonderfully made: marvellous are thy works; and that my soul knoweth right well. My substance was not hid from thee, when I was made in secret, and curiously wrought in the lowest parts of the earth. Thine eyes did see my substance, yet being unperfect; and in thy book all my members were written, which in continuance were fashioned, when as yet there was none of them. How precious also are thy thoughts unto me, O God! How great is the sum of them!

PSALM 139:12–17, KJV

Chapter one

Birth

It all begins with birth. Birth is the emergence of the bud. The powerful début of life is seen in the drama of birth. The grand entrée into the world of a frail-looking, much protesting offspring is an experience that words fail to capture precisely. The baby's cry, the confirmation of life, heralds an overflow of rejoicing.

Birth is a paradoxical moment. When a child is born, parents are born. For a mother especially, each birth is a new experience, awakening afresh the process of motherhood. Irrespective of the number of birth experiences of a woman, the arrival of each offspring evokes a singular response of love and nurture in her heart, honor to the unique individuality of the newborn.

Birth is a moment of triumph. The wailing, vernix-covered, scrounged-up, bewildered infant is the symbol of victory, the trophy to be proudly displayed by both parents after many months of suspense. Birth transforms the wearied, sweat-adorned, slightly confused mother into a portrait of joy and gratitude, while the formerly agitated father changes into a hulk of fiery pride, coated in dazed emotions.

Birth is a moment where the balance of life is held in momentary limbo. It is that precise point in time that pierces through the moment, redefining the word *normalcy* through the marvelous presence of life.

Birth is God's gifting of continuity.

The parents are overwhelmed by their swaddling gift of innocence, a gift whose soft features convey a gentle message of helplessness. Toothless gums revealed in unprovoked smiles, startled eyes trailing moves in seeming expectation, little hands gripping the air firmly or a finger in a trusting clutch; fuzzy head burrowing instinctively into the croon of the arm for a feed…innocence is a person, a fresh bud of life.

The new parents are filled with wonderment at their newly birthed daughter. They christen her Flower.

The natural course of events makes the gestation period one filled with much expectation, and the air is condensed with excited preparation!

Unfortunately, sometimes the natural course of events is broken, and what happens is an exception toeing an unnatural course. These exceptions are often clouded in painful experiences where thorns of anguish prick the hallway of the affected person's life. Children conceived in the horror of the human depravity of rape or incest, children whose mothers were neither consulted nor their consent sought in their formation, line life's corridor. Children, conceived in insidious circumstances, products of a moment of wanton lust, often walk the streets in bottled rage. A growing fetus cocooned in a womb of anger is at risk, apparently shielded from external stimuli but receiving direct nurture in rebounds of hurt and pain from an unforgiveness-saturated abode. Inevitably the growing fetus is incubated in a climate of lovelessness, a hollow of denial and rejection.

Sadly, in this present society seemingly sold out to perversion, this appears increasingly to be the mindless legacy we are set to leave the next generation.

If the above depiction comes anything close to your situation, and your background as a phantom incessantly dogs your heels, don't let the pain of your past make your present puerile and unproductive. You must understand that although the circumstances of your birth might not have evoked the naturally intended joy, nevertheless, God was affected by your birth. He was thrown into excitement at your arrival because He was involved in the process of your creation from the outset! "Why then would He have allowed the background of my birth to be so traumatic?" I hear someone ask in anguish. I don't have all the answers. However, there might be a parallel in that just the same way God allows people make a choice for hell though He has lavishly prepared the joys of heaven, likewise He can be seemingly powerless in averting a lineup of sordid events leading to a traumatic conception—particularly if no middle person was interceding in prayer on behalf of either the victim or the predator of the calamity. God has given man the distinctive gift of a free will, and with this, man must bear the responsibility of his choices. Either he reaps a reward or a punishment; there is no middle walk.

You can blot out the nightmare of your past by turning over your pain to Jesus[1] and allowing him bring stability and balance to your life. Enter into the brisk walk of life with the realization that you are not an accident of nature but the singular workmanship of God's artistry.

I'd like to wrap this up by reminding you that God carefully monitored your growth within the womb.[2] God checked that all your body parts were recorded, and then He went on ahead to make them, to fashion them.

When we talk fashion, a designer comes to mind. Designers don't do a hasty job. They take their time. God took His time with you. He structured your nose to be that size and that mold, and He taped your ears exactly as He wished them to be by the sides of your head. You are exclusively crafted. You are not an accident of nature but a gift to humanity. When as yet none of your features were recognizable and you were but a fertilized egg dividing and

---

1   "Therefore if any man be in Christ, he is a new creature: old things are passed away; behold, all things are become new" (2 Corinthians 5:17).
2   "...in thy book all my members were written, which in continuance were fashioned" (Psalm 139:16).

redividing to form a cluster of cells, God was directly involved in the process! Psalm 139:17 culminates your importance in the words, "How precious also are thy thoughts unto me, O God."

You have to believe the Holy Book because it is true! You can never begin to actualize yourself and fulfill your God-given purpose and destiny on Earth until you connect with the Author of life. No man is adequately placed to foretell your destiny because no man stands in the place of Creator. You are not the person anyone says you are because nobody has an authoritative insight into your full potential. The restrictive limitations borne out of fleshly minds will at best offer only a myopic perspective of your abilities. You are more than you presently believe you are, gifted far beyond your own imagination. The only way you can rightfully come to the point of purpose is by coming to terms with God the Creator.[3]

"How precious also are thy thoughts unto me, O God!" *Precious* means, "dear, cherished, very costly or valuable, held in high esteem." God does not think any mean thoughts about you. He holds you in high esteem and preserves a treasure of thoughts of you. You are the crown of His creation.[4]

With this understanding, the cruel, misleading, piercing, and hurtful words thrown at you over the years should no longer shape your future. Reject them as willful untruths, an incorrect representation of your person. "Misfit, good-for-nothing, hopeless, useless, clumsy, daft, a pain, thorn-in-the-flesh, black sheep, an excuse to humanity, no good..." Are there other wicked and demeaning words? Now is the time to add them to this limited catalog and trash them accordingly. I enjoin you to do this cleansing exercise and put the hurt and the aches of the past behind you forever. Take a plain sheet of paper and pen down all the negative counts that have been leveled against you and attributed to your person; do this

---

3   "Jesus saith unto him, I am the way, the truth, and the life: no man cometh unto the Father, but by me" (John 14:6).

4   "For I know the thoughts that I think toward you, saith the Lord, thoughts of peace, and not of evil, to give you an expected end" (Jeremiah 29:11).

with a firm determination of releasing them and relinquishing their hold forever upon your life.

As you begin to write, the cleansing will commence. Read out every noun and adjective you have written, and as you give voice to your pain, make this bold statement to seal your freedom:

> I neither am nor represent any of these evil lies penned down and even those that come to mind this moment. I am fearfully and wonderfully made by God the Creator, my Maker. Jesus came to redeem me and restore me. Through this knowledge I declare that I am the redeemed of the Lord, and in faith I say that today I am restored to wholesomeness. This day I put a stop to Satan's lies in my life as I align my thoughts to agree with God's declaration of who I am. I am God's treasured possession, the apple of His eyes, His holy nation. I am created in God's image. His image is resplendent with love. The earth is more blessed by my presence, and I give God all the glory as I change the picture in my mind to align with the picture in God's mind. I am fearfully and wonderfully made. Thank You, Lord! In Jesus's name, amen.

The mirror of God's heartbeat desire is the Holy Bible. Peer into it and begin to see expressions of the depth of His love. The references below are some illustrations of His compassionate nature and the power of His love for you, His most cherished and treasured possession.

God says that you are:

- His portion and the apple of His eye (Deuteronomy 32:9–10)
- The head and not the tail (Deuteronomy 28:13)
- More than a conqueror (Romans 8:37)
- Chosen, royal, holy, and peculiar (1 Peter 2:9)

Make the above your identity statement until you are so fully persuaded you are able to add to it, "And that my soul knows right well." In this, indeed, is the affirmation that you know beyond a shadow of doubt—within you as well as without—that you've got Almighty God's stamp of approval on you!

A glimpse of God's loving nature is depicted in the verse that states, "[God] hast covered me in my mother's womb" (Psalm 139:13). His overwhelming protection and care are revealed in His concern for you right within the unseen realm of your mother's womb. Your very existence is for a purpose. Begin to bear your life as a badge of honor to humanity, and no longer hide in a hermit's cocoon.

Chapter two

Innocence

THE INITIAL FLUTTERY picture of arrival soon settles into the reality of a fresh routine with much added activity. Suddenly, the canvas of mother's life is painted upon with bold strokes of intrusion splayed over its former background of serenity. Her once carefully planned life is now forever forfeited to fit a fresh style: a new baby-centered cycle.

Each spurt of Flower's growth brings acclaims of joy and encouragement. Each stage is greeted with "oohs" and "aahs," lavish shows of appreciation. Flower grows progressively and so impressively! She gurgles with joy as her sitting posture is applauded. She struggles earnestly to coax her body to respond to vain attempts to move: little arms flaying the air and chubby legs kicking! It is with surprise that she discovers that movement is achieved with body raised and not tummy grounded. Somewhat momentarily startled, she suddenly realizes that she is moving! Jerky, nonetheless coordinated, moves. Her rapturous cries are a pure delight to the ear! Yet too soon Flower is dissatisfied with the status quo and begins novel attempts at further advancement. She prods herself up and maintains a shaky balance as she stands. Confidence builds, and Flower takes her first step. Mother's encouragement propels her on while father's excitement stimulates her. Pleased, she plants one stocky leg west of the other pointed northeast.

Strangely, although brimming over with love for this infant, mother sometimes finds herself as in a battlefield divide. She is taken aback by sudden sweeping emotional resentments against

Flower, who ironically represents the very center of her natural motherly instincts of affection. She struggles with the frustration evoked by unexpected surges of annoyance, and the aftermath invasion of a debilitating, overwhelming sense of remorse that mocks at her and derides her ability to be a good mother!

Few mothers would confess to nursing uncomplimentary feelings toward their offspring, feelings when the "little blessing" is viewed as the "little brat"! When a demanding cry from the cot is the last straw threatening to break the fragile thread of mother's residual patience, she swallows up her irritation in chokes of guilt. A freshly diapered baby soils the diaper anew, and it would do mother a world of relief to crumble into tears for a few seconds before laughing at the absurdity of the incident. Unfortunately, most times she plays Super Mom on the outside while inwardly she sobs her heart out. Sometimes the mountain of chores plus baby needs plus dinner preparation looms up before her, and she is convinced that Mount Everest would be a much easier exploit to undertake. Rather than make the healthy choice to command the problems to line up and take turns for her attention, she clams shut her mouth to stem the impending hysteria. Then with stoic resolve and a heavy heart, she trudges on through the dreary doldrums of another demanding day. Super Mom is speedily degenerating into a dangerous time bomb set to go off. She is walking on a delicate tightrope that needs a balance of laughter and venting for a return to stability.

Although real times of utter tension and desperation exist, the intense scenario can be softened by cultivating a correct mind-set and positive self-discipline. To see the beauty in every situation, mother must learn not to take herself too seriously. Baby making a mess of her freshly diapered backside should cause a good laugh! All babies do the big J (job) at the wrong time. But you have to believe that to all intents and purposes, there is no malice intended!

Innocence

Innocence must be recognized as being demanding in its dependency. The newborn, neither corrupted nor tainted with evil, is harmless, blameless, and pure. However, the infant's vulnerability represents for the caretakers the epitome of dependency. The baby is dependent on another person for aid, support, and life. This dependency beams an enormous responsibility on those assigned with the role of active caring. It requires the combination of sensitivity and wisdom to successfully manage a balance between home and baby responsibilities.

A woman cooped up all day with her baby and the seeming never-ending cycle of baby-related needs—such as bathe baby, dress baby, feed baby, burp baby—can rightfully feel a little nutty within a short space of time. Usually, when that cycle is broken, it is only for a brief interlude in order to accommodate a similar one: boil water for baby's bottle, change baby's sterilized water, soak baby's soiled diaper in sanitized water, wash, dry, iron, do baby's laundry!

There is no need to panic or to feel frantic. God has equipped and fitted women perfectly for the mental, emotional, and physical challenges of both the tasking and fulfilling role of motherhood. No matter how inept the new mother feels, she has been endued from above with the grace to fulfill her motherhood role with uncanny and unbeatable expertise, that would shame the most bookish expert spouting distrustful theories! Motherhood is challenging, but motherhood is also fun! It is a blessing from God, and His blessing enriches, with no sorrow added to it!

Many mothers would admit to enjoying the periods of dependency exhibited by their child and feeling a little nostalgic when independence begins to tug at the reins of the relationship and the child shows signs of curiosity and boldness to venture out alone. In the same breath, though, mother finds a degree of relief in her semi-independence release.

Prior to the separation that comes with independence, every now and again the demands become overwhelming, and mother urgently needs help. Other times she needs to *get out*. Literally, she needs to get out of the house for a breath of refreshing air. When she does succeed in an outing, it may appear as a travesty, for within a short spell, mother assumes a new dirge in the form of a gentle whine of "I miss my baby," "I wonder how my baby is doing?", and finally, "When are we going back home [to my baby])?" These are unspoken, yet implied.

It takes a heavy dose of understanding for the father not to be exasperated by these contradictions in his normally more predictable wife. Father is an integral part in ensuring that stability and harmony are preserved in the home. Many are oblivious to the enormous demands the little innocent makes on mother and how powerfully through yells, wails, screams, and tears her emotions are manipulated till she finally gives in to the whims and caprices of the little one. It takes wisdom to guard against allowing baby's hollering to become an instrument of control.

Father's assistance, always appreciated, becomes even more so when he is available to help outside the baby-perfect-times where baby is presented as the little angel. (These are those times when baby is clean, powdered, diapered, dolled, and fed!) When father rolls up his sleeves and makes a mess of the bath in an attempt to successfully give baby a bath, or emerges victorious after a grueling feed time with gooey baby food intermeshed in his hair, or treads a beaten path in the carpet through pacing to and fro, diligently trying to work out a burp from a food-sedated infant, or finally tries to lull baby to sleep on the mattress of his tummy, himself nodding off—applaud his efforts and appreciate him with much fanfare!

The following three words of advice to maintain harmony in the home should be observed by both parents, but more so by the father: "Break the cycle!" To keep the love flow pipe unclogged and enjoy the peace of still waters (see Psalm 23:3), it is crucial that the cycle of normalcy be continuously broken.

Innocence

Break the cycle.

Husband, find someone to babysit for one to three hours, and take your wife out. It doesn't have to be an expensive outing. Getting an ice cream treat or a roasted fish and plantain native eat will do. Irrelevant the where, relevant the act—just the two of you, alone, somewhere.

Break the cycle.

Husband, take both mother and baby out. Visit friends who will be honored to have "little adorable" in their home. With them sure to fawn all over baby, mother is able to put her feet up and relax as she is waited upon!

Break the cycle.

Husband, volunteer to stay home and look after baby while mom goes out with the girls for a leisure break. (My husband once did so, and I happily escaped. On my return, I learned that baby had done a major job in her diaper, but dad had been quick to the rescue! With nearly an entire roll of tissue depleted, baby was labeled "CLEAN.")

Break the cycle.

Husband, flatter your wife's esteem. Be sensitive to any voiced request (within limits—*you* determine the limits), and spoil her. Buy her something unique and memorable (not pots and pans, something especially for her... for her!). Spend a little of that hard-earned cash on her! Celebrate her!

Break the cycle.

Husband, phone your wife from work. Tell her how special she is; crown it by telling her not to fix dinner, as you will bring dinner home from a local restaurant.

Break the cycle.

Break the cycle.

Break the cycle.

The results of breaking the cycle are amazing! Modest acts

saturated with love impact beyond the stretch of imagination. For a more lovable wife and able mother, for a more stable, relaxed, and welcome home, apply three words: break the cycle!

Chapter three

Not So Innocent

THE FEMALE'S AREA of strength is in her power to influence. God has placed immense deposits of power in the female; the magnitude of her influence is giddying to imagine.

The Bible is resplendent with female figures that have graced history with the priceless jewels of their person. The Ruths, Esthers, Elizabeths, and Marys have proven a tribute to womanhood. Similarly, infamous women as Jezebel, Delilah, and Herodias have equally spotted the annals of history with their persons.

What is this non-tangible known as influence?

It is the effect of a person or thing over another. Broadened a little bit, it is the power of one person or thing to have such an effect. Influence could be earthed in a person's ability, wealth, position, or personality. We all exercise influence over different audiences and in varying degrees: a mother to her daughter; a father to his son, teacher to pupil, doctor to patient, chairman to company, president to nation, and so on.

Influence is the *power to affect*.

Let's peek in on Flower.

She now scoots all over the place on confident little legs, establishing her quest for independence. She is communicating fairly well in baby babble and is just as adorable as she is innocent. Innocent?

There is an ingraining process that occurs in a child through the fawning of family and friends. For a girl, cries such as "Isn't she beautiful?" are constant punctuation marks embedding themselves into her young psyche in the earliest days.

For Flower, this feedback has been an incessant playback from proud parents who have been overwhelming in acknowledging their daughter in positive affirmations. With this healthy nurture, her self-esteem has grown with remarkable ease. Every furniture mountain is a challenge to surmount, and with amazing confidence she conquers each in victorious climbs. The hunger for discovery draws her to the bed drawers as she forages through them in impulsive treasure hunts. Such adventures spurred by curiosity do not evoke a reprimand from father and mother. Invisible walls of security spring up about her with every voiced encouragement.

Flower's parents are careful to balance their daughter's sense of self-worth in the light of God's Word, thus protecting her from being whipped up in an egotistic pool of narcissistic love. The parental assurance open to her protects her from the deceit of flattery, and she is settled in knowing that she is "God's gift," a baby beauty needing no further proof in tot beauty pageants.

Flower's excesses in adorning herself in her mother's tops and scarves, loading her young neck with strings of beads, losing her feet in the hollows of mother's shoes, and smudging her lips and cheek with lipstick are all the natural response to influence. In such acts she replays what she has learned through observation.

Flower stumbles into the discovery of her femininity. Intuitively she learns and acts out the subtleties of her femaleness. Just as when in the crib she discovered crying as her number one power tool, wielding it with wild abandon, Flower begins to understand without any explanation that she possesses another power! In the crib, staccato shrills commanded immediate attention. With whining wails she won her way, while fretful crying forced irritation to condescend to some level of consideration by others. Those diaper days were filled with divergent manipulative tactics. Alas!

Not So Innocent

Mother caught on much too quickly, and soon enough Flower's nearly unfettered cacophonous days were brought to an end.

At five years of age, Flower is a gem. Her loveliness is highlighted not only in ribbons and bows but also in her sweet disposition. Playful and carefree, curious and questioning, she is a pure delight! Flower has had to learn to conform to home rules. Whenever she strays from the set borders of liberty, father and mother are faithful to administer the rod in correction. Not for Flower a public display of tantrums: throwing herself on the floor, making a scene to have her way. Once tried, twice wiser. In a desperate attempt to have her parents buy something she wanted, Flower resorted to an ACT (A-Class Tantrum). Flinging herself down onto the supermarket floor, she began a berserk fit of anger. Father's response was swift and unexpected. In one fell swoop he picked her up, tucked her firmly under his arm, and marched out of the store with head held high and mother close by his steps. She was bundled into the car on a homeward drive. The ride home was heavy with father's palpable displeasure. Once through the safe enclosure of the walled fence and within the private confines of the home, the roots of her decadent behavior were exorcised without delay. From the bashful corner emerged a strident cane. In three succinct strokes father articulated the chastisement. The flexible stick made contact upon the bedded posterior of Flower's anatomy, and oh, how she wailed! But oh, did she learn! Swift were the strokes, distinct the sting, clear the message, and instant the repentance!

Not for Flower were pouts and outbursts in the bid to get her way. The years have proven to her the pointlessness in pursuing a nagging and stubbornly insistent path. She has learned slowly but surely that compliance is the surer way of achieving results. She has come to understand that the more obedient she shows herself, the greater confidence father and mother place in her. To acts of obedience are much applause and more encouragement. Preferred is this response over a scold, a reproach, or a denial altogether.

Flower's growth is scented with a natural sweetness borne

of growing in the safe nest of loving discipline. The aura of her femininity is seen in the halo of her childish charm. Flower's words are polite and her gestures gracious. Her presentation in speech is adorned with flutters of "please," "may I," and "thank you." Unwittingly, she gets her way. The power of her femininity is embedded in the treasure of her submissiveness. Her attitude is gentle, yielding, and non-confrontational. Sparkling character jewels of Flower's person are being slowly revealed, priceless nuggets of charisma.

How could a mother not melt at the words, "Mommy dear…" or be touched by the tender voiced offer of help with chubby outstretched hands, volunteering, "Let Flower wash plate for mommy!" What father would not respond to love expressed in putty fingers patting a head of thinning hair, herald of premature balding? What father would remain unaffected by the planting of a kiss on his oily forehead? How could a father remain untouched by those precious four words gushed in tender child tones, "Daddy, I love you."

Too often adults play a diminutive part in the child's growth; they are guilty of caging the child's thinking to fit within firmly bounded stereotypes. They act in ignorance, underestimating the child's capability to understand and express intelligence in rational and logical terms. A child's natural inclination at communication can be hampered and hushed through an adult's wrong response. The child depends on example in order to respond likewise through mimicry. If the example followed is substandard, what is reproduced will naturally be substandard. Adults imagine that they need to descend to infantile levels when communicating with little children. What they miss is that *infantile* must be defined. By nature, every child is a copier, mimicking and reproducing words and actions heard and observed. Where the diet fed is gibberish, the reproduced utterances and mimicked gestures are the same. Also, the less a child is spoken to, the weaker the vocabulary exhibited. The purity of vocabulary is much affected by the manner in which words are spoken. This implies that the infant who is spoken to in terms of babble will respond likewise. Growth at this stage is extremely reliant. For children's lives to be affected positively, they must have good role models who appreciate and regard children as thinking beings who possess the bona fide rights of full grown citizens. Minors acting grown up are interesting to behold! They innocently carry on their little antics projecting through replays role models who have captured their young hearts. Adults, in recognizing the power of influence they exert on young lives, are to act with a near reverent sense of responsibility.

Indeed, the atmosphere of a little girl's growth is unconsciously framed to bring attention to her. Also perfectly normal and desirable are feeding her young heart's desire for positive acclaims. Who best to offer approval than those most valuable to her—dad and mom? Phrasings evaluating the externals of her person ought to be emphasized in line with the invisible internal person—the carrier of principles and virtues. Within her is bred a sense of discernment that renders her innocuous to the tottering dictates of her sensibilities. As a result of a healthy self-esteem foundation, she will be able to keep her own and stand her ground in the future when confronted with negatives regarding her physique. Cozy in God, confident of His goodness, and sure of His promises, she cannot be deceived into believing an unwholesome and deprecatory self-assessment.

God does not fear a boomerang "big-head" effect resulting from loving, encouraging words spoken to His children. He knows that His creations require a regular dose of healthy, positive words to guarantee their development and the cultivation of a good self-image. We ought to follow His example.

As a child, my father was in the habit of pulling my nose under the pretext that he wanted to ensure that I "grew" a long, straight nose. This act registered an opposite message to my brain—basically that I did not have the desired nose type and therefore was somewhat at a disadvantage. I was convinced that his attempts to belatedly correct my nose proved a further affirmation of my handicap. In fact, in dad's dogged attempts to "fix" my nose was the glaring implication that all other nose types outside the above described kind was defective.

This kind of skewed thinking was characteristic of my childhood, and it followed me into much of my growing-up days. Clearly etched in my mind are other incidents. At about the time I was spiraling between the ages of three and four, I was consumed with an excessive interest in my looks. Positioned before the dressing mirror in my mother's room, I would plaster my face with layers of talcum powder from what seemed to me a gigantic powder bowl with an equally sized powder puff! My preoccupation with my face grew. At age seven a vivid event occurred that brought a distant God close to my semi-heathen heart.

A magnificent mirror towered in the hallway of our then villa abode nested in the suburbs of Paris. Each time I passed by it, I could not help but be momentarily transfixed by my reflection. I would stare with intense admiration at the charming beauty who looked back at me. At that early age I was able to find flaws to criticize the perfection of God's handiwork. (I was convinced that I had bags under my young eyes and terrified that in my childhood, I was going to be prematurely transformed into looking like the many gray-haired old ladies in the neighborhood.) On this one occasion, as I admired and appreciated myself, a thought scuttled across my mind. I grabbed the scurrying thought and wrestled with it in a bid to firmly place it in my mind's hold. As I pondered a little about the subject, I internally nodded agreement with my thoughts. I was desirous and deserving of a vacation! Thoughts of truancy began to race within the confines of my mind, doing mild somersaults against the walls, bouncing back into the center of my brain for the opportunity of a second consideration. Alas! I had to release them, knowing fully well that I couldn't quite get past my punctilious father had I the courage to transmute the deviant thoughts into deviant acts! Yet another thought sped wildly through my mind, and this I caught in mid-flight! This just might work (*if only...*). I voiced out my wish quite unbelieving, yet desiring it intensely. I specified my request carefully before God... something to this effect: "Please, God, make me a little sick so that I am unable to go to school and can stay home for about five days."

The devil, not God, caught on to this perverted prayer and willingly obliged me. (Imagine a willing candidate for sickness?) No bars reserved age-wise, the imps delivered their gift with impious promptness. The very next day I woke up, and as I passed my favorite image reflector of "Who's the prettiest of them all?," I was dumbfounded to discover that I was covered over with an awful rash. Panic gripped my young heart as I stood aghast, studying this spectered face with weird mole-like bumps spread all over. My repentance was immediate, and supplications followed right behind. Scared stiff that I would be left with the ravage of the damage of permanent scars upon my delicate person, I began earnestly to renegotiate with God, whom I foolishly credited as the source of this benign evil. From all rational observations, my prayer went unanswered. The devil had got me cheap—by a personal foolish invitation—and he just wasn't about to let me off without having his fill of malicious mischief and fiendish fun. It took the scourge a five-day stretch before elapsing.

Vanity is the quality of being vain. Webster's dictionary defines *vain* as "thinking too highly of one's appearance, attainments." Contrast this against the Word of God, which states in Romans 12:3, "I warn everyone among you not to estimate and think of himself more highly than he ought [not to have an exaggerated opinion of his own importance], but to rate his ability with sober judgment" (AMP). In essence, the lesson is not a caution to estimate and think highly of yourself, but to discern vanity and to rip it at the budding stage.

While careful not to poison or destroy the individual's sense of self-worth, one should nonetheless beware a mental diet laid over with coats of vanity and iced in bloats of flattery. Bring up your little girl in the safe enclosure of approval and acceptance, and her self-esteem will rise. She has been fearfully and wonderfully made!

Part II

Blossom

What? know ye not that your body is the temple of the Holy Ghost which is in you, which ye have of God, and ye are not your own? For ye are bought with a price: therefore glorify God in your body, and in your spirit, which are God's.

1 Corinthians 6:19–20

Chapter four

Seasons of Change

THE LINE NETWORK embedded on mother's stomach is the unique aftermath signature pointing to Flower's abode for nine months. The nest of the womb was the home where Flower's dependency on mother was at its peak. Mother's once youthful svelteness has forever been displaced by perceptible, telltale touches of fat deposits cozily nested on her person. Life is about change and growth, and each passing year brings forth season's seedlings—irrepressible and insuppressible growth. Flower's conception and birth ushered fresh seasons of change in mother's life.

Mother and Flower simultaneously experienced change. To be acquainted with body changes is to be prepared to accept them.

About the age of nine, the bud begins to unfold its tender petals in emerging blossom. A petal totters and curves outwards in awakening breasts. Another petal comes forth in the pubes and hair in armpits. Yet another petal uncurls, shrinking back baby fat to be reproduced (it would seem), as fat deposits lodged on the hips. Of distinct significance is the spreading of yet another petal in the menstrual cycle.

Seasons of change! How precious for a mother to cultivate with her daughter a special closeness! How vital to share with her in confidence stages of growing up even before she is thus grown!

How necessary to be her friend, expounding the treasures of her unfolding person and bridging any stream of confusion that may rise! How important to be able to extend a guiding hand of love to her when needed the most!

A girl stands on the threshold of womanhood, and she peeks into her femininity. Curious and confused, excited and apprehensive, she stands at a crossroad. She is an exquisite treasury! Within her costly array is a pearl of great value. Innocent of this knowledge, unsuspecting and unknowing, how is she to esteem and care for the pearl? She may guard it carefully or handle it carelessly. She may preserve it or shrug it off, tossing it aside unconcernedly. She may hide it quietly or flaunt it openly. Precious and priceless is the pearl in her possession. Will she protect it, or will she peddle it? This pearl of great value is her virginity. This is her birth gift from God, the seal of her chastity, a seal that must remain unbroken until marriage! Only in the legal estate of marriage is she at liberty to give up this pearl, which then may be relinquished with joy and pride on the night of her wedding to the love of her life. In a moment of love the delicate traverse from girlhood to womanhood is then completed.

Yet even as the bud spreads out in blossom, weeds spring up and vie for the contended prize—the pearl of virginity. They contest the blossom's turf and pose an incessant attack on her. They draw life from the soil's goodness, aiming to weaken the blossom and dry up the sap of her life through stolen peace and joy, premature heralds of death. The weeds are a threat so dangerous that they must be uprooted quickly, speedily, immediately! It is reckless and unwise to permit them time to fix their roots firmly into the earth.

The world, from bowels of wickedness, vomits indigestible villainy in an effort to underrate the inestimable worth of the pearl. The pearl of virginity is trifled, chastity is demeaned, and purity is openly vilified. With this trend, an unsuspecting and naïve lass may easily be tricked into doing away with her priceless pearl, allowing it to be sullied and stained. However, with the foundational understanding of her body being God's temple, an awe of reverence surrounds the blossoming maiden so that she guards her body with holy jealousy.

Though weeds spring up in stubborn persistence, discernment will reveal the weeds of evil's deceit, and immediately, they must be crushed.

> Evil beckons in mischief's cloak of deceit.
> Beware the voice smooth as polished granite
> Pouring out promises resoundingly hollow
> Making vows extremely shallow
> Urging you in oily undertones
> To part with your pearl.
> Sweet he says are waters stol'n
> But stolen waters[5] though sweet at first
> At the end, birth intense pain, deep within.
>
> Evil beckons in mischief's cloak of deceit.
> Beware…in array of presents,
> Varied and tantalizing
> Outwardly appealing
> Inwardly demeaning
> These are nought but gilded gifts
> Baited snares to trap you with
> Don't fall for the lies, they are truncated stumps
> Holding within nothing of comparable worth…
> "Special," he says, "are the gifts I bring."
> But to pluck out your pearl is the desire hid with'n.
>
> Evil beckons in mischief's cloak of deceit.
> Beware…a feast is laid and drinks overflow
> In much jocundity an' merriment
> Sense easily sways to sensuality

---

[5] "Bread of deceit is sweet to a man; but afterwards his mouth shall be filled with gravel" (Proverbs 20:17).

In orgy of eating and excess of drinking
The mind slurred turns to a blur.
Be self-controlled and even tempered.
Be vigilant, watch out, the enemy's on the prowl.
For a morsel of food and a swallow of drink
Forcefully he intends to pry out the pearl!

Evil beckons in mischief's cloak of deceit.
But stronger the strength is purity's poise
A shield of protection, celest' tested words.
In knowledge and understanding,
Walls of wisdom withstand
The lies, the deceit, the poisonous charm.
The temple unharmed; the enemy foiled,
Shamed, sullen, surly slinks away
Beware evil's allure.
Stay pure.

The physical changes evoke a conflict scenario between the body and the mind. The mind is at variance with the sprouts of femininity in body form, and unless a bridge of understanding is built through knowledge, a void may be left, resulting in confusion.

What is Flower to do with the daily eruptions caused by hormonal activity that produce geometric body changes to her person? The growth avalanche nudges to wakefulness her sexuality. So many questions knock at her brain. Questions, many questions, and more questions! Some of the questions tugging at her heart are so...private? And *silly*? No, absolutely ridiculous! How much more convenient it would be to act as if they didn't matter, but that in itself would be a parody of self-deception. She mentally plays a scenario where she consults with her friends and is educated by them...or would it be more appropriate to say "initiated into a circle of speculative thinking"? And rather than come out clean in their ignorance, they might attempt through banter to conceal the depth of their gaucherie in details private and sensitive. Intuitively, she knows that help from them would most likely leave her more confused at the close of much prater. Pondering her options, mother's face looms at her. She starts with a grin! Of course, mother is the key! With mother, her ignorance would be safe and received with understanding and without ado. Her ineptness would be given much kindness, great patience, and loving respect.

Dissimulations and denials from parents in this fragile period of growth are just as destructive as the young girl's assumptions are lethal. Parents must be willing and ready to answer the tugging questions on sex and sexuality. Bashful innuendoes resolve nothing.

Seasons of change roll out a whole new volley of vocabulary from the language vault. Brassieres, deodorants, sanitary napkins, tampons, perfumes, makeup, hair styles…

Seasons of change excite experimentation. Trials are attempted in bra sizes, deodorant types, makeup mixes, choice of monthly hygiene napkin or tampon.

Seasons of change blow out puffs of knowledge. Independence is perched on young shoulders and youth, inclined to boast, tries to prove its gradual growth to be completed growth! Love teaches the difference. The smart "know-it-all" young lady is often inclined to leap into reckless experimentation. Maturity, on the other hand, displays its superior character in traits of caution and care.

Young girl, be tranquil and listen to the experience of the older woman. Listen carefully to your mother, for her advice is stringed in love. With her by your side, you will make the right discoveries at the right time. Safe in the cove of mother's love, you will walk through potentially dangerous roads with protected ease.

God's commandments are not burdensome…parental restrictions are not a deprivation.

Be perceptive and discern the strings of love in parental interest of your whereabouts—though you feel it to be busybody monitoring, they are simply strings of love.

Be perceptive and discern the strings of love in parent-imposed curfews—you feel it's an infringement on your liberty, but they are simply strings of love.

Be perceptive and discern the strings of love in your parents' voiced disapproval of some of your friends, and hearken when they advise you to cut loose those relationships—you may feel it's uncalled-for interference, but they are simply strings of love.

Be perceptive and discern the strings of love in parents' strict orders to attend optional church activities—you may feel your independence is being restricted, but they are simply strings of love.

Be perceptive and discern the strings of love in blatant parental disagreement at some course of action you plan to undertake—you feel the lack of support proves a lack of confidence in your ability to make decisions, but they are simply strings of love.

Young girl, listen carefully to your mother, for her advice is stringed in love. Don't rely on your feelings, for feelings are as fleeting and flighty as the fickle passage of your moods.

Chapter five

Crossing

VARIOUS PHYSICAL, EMOTIONAL, and mental changes have come in waves and ebbed into gentle tides of normalcy, but Flower remains at a loss, for a vital petal in her formation is still curled in. She feels incomplete in her physiological makeup, an outsider from her peers who all have, at age seventeen, crossed the symbolic threshold from girlhood into womanhood through the menstrual flow.

To some, Flower is fortunate. Her parents who view the physical and spiritual benefits of the menstrual cycle are discomfited by the delay. Trying not to appear overly concerned, mother codes the question for what seems to Flower the umpteenth time in the week. "Anything yet, dear?" Her excessive fretting annoys Flower, who crossly walks past her without a reply. "What is the big deal!" she explodes inwardly. Her friends are happy for her; her parents are worried. And she is confused and feels lacking! This crossroad conflict with her in the spotlight is, to say the least, disconcerting. Shutting the door behind her in her room, she leans back on it and with eyes cast upward in a plea, she prays, "Dear Lord, just make them all mind their business!" Then, sighing, she whispers, "But anyway, what *is* the matter with me?"

Finally, unable to bear the pressure any longer, she seeks professional counsel and pays a visit to the gynecologist. Submitting all the fluid samples requested for tests to be run, she returns a week later for her next appointment. The doctor is fatherly and looks understanding. After a brief consultative chat, he looks through the various reports and her medical file. Seated in his plum chair, he nods to himself. An anxious Flower follows his every movement with her eyes and awaits his verdict. To his kind assuring smile, her apprehensive state allows her to return only a fraction of a fugitive smile. When finally he assures her that she is perfectly normal and needs only to be patient and wait for the flow to start, Flower is overcome with the conflicting emotions of relief and disappointment. She begins to shake her head, refusing the doctor's pat response as the final verdict. Close to the brink of tears, she pleads to be given some drugs, a helping hand to stop this waiting. It is apparent to the doctor that her distress is real, and he yields in a compromise gesture, scribbling a prescription for a regimen of drugs that purportedly could help induce the flow. Placated, Flower is ready to leave. At the door, the doctor calls back. Peering over the borderless rim of his glasses, he ventures a parting shot. "Nothing abnormal," he says. "It's just a matter of time." Hastily Flower steps out and shuts the door against this most erudite opinion.

It takes two and a half weeks of committed pill popping without any noticeable change, aside from a horrible harvest of acne on her face, to convince Flower that the doctor was right. Clearly frustrated and fed up, she flushes the remaining medication in her possession down the toilet.

The menstrual cycle's entrée into a young girl's life is often without fanfare or any noticeable sign. For some, the advent of the cycle is relatively early—as early as nine years; for others, it may be so much later—as late as nineteen! I would say, as I give it some thought, my case was one of being smitten.

In the eleventh year of my life I grew up suddenly! I had an avidity for books that was fueled by a dose of self-pride. Having recently become a proud library member, I couldn't make enough trips to and from the library, borrowing and returning and borrowing books anew! It was an extremely rewarding experience to be able to go to the library and use my library card to check out books all by myself. Of course, this opportunity to show off over and over again greatly increased my appetite for reading!

I was at "The End'" part of a story that left me as ignorant as I was prior to reading it, if not a little more bewildered and perplexed. Now, I was saddled with the task of trying to piece together the puzzle of the story. Two little girls (more scamps than ladies) were involved in some teenage mischief. As they pondered their naughtiness and its possible repercussions, their "playful prank" began to take on a tangy taste. Overtaken with remorse, they sought refuge in a nearby church where they planned to get the weight off their chests. The first girl, with heartfelt repentance, knelt to pray. The second, about to follow suit, stood transfixed in shocked disbelief as she stared at a visible spread of red on her friend's outfit. She cried out in horror, "Sin has broken out all over you!" For the map of red was indeed blood. Terrified by this immediate act of retribution from above, they both fled home in near hysteria.

Sin was a term unknown to me at the time of reading, and the whole narration proved totally incomprehensible. It took a couple of months later for me to make the connection in the story when I became the center of another drama. "Sin" broke out of my body, and near hysteria came close in its step! I recount...

It was not an unusual evening. Returning home from my bicycle ride, I parked my bike by the house and went indoors. I needed to use the bathroom in a rush! I was absolutely unprepared for the sight that met my eyes. What was this dark red flush on my pants? Instinctively I knew it was blood. I was terrified! How did it happen? Why did it happen? What had I done to merit this evil? My mind went on an auto-reverse of the day's entire happenings. "What wickedness had I committed?" I thought frantically. Totally frightened, I forced my brain to *think*. It was useless! I couldn't answer the why. I needed to suppress and hopefully stop the flow. But how? "A bath should do it," I reasoned. I took a bath, but there was no stopping the sluggish flow of red.

I was in big trouble. There was no hiding place.

I knew I had to talk to someone quickly. My imagination went on a fast-forward projectile into the future. My mind encapsulated a histrionic story line set ahead into time. How would my doting father take this? He would be heartbroken, I reckoned. I imagined how I would try to allay his fears…how stoic I would be. I would smile bravely while strapped to the stretcher, and the medics would whisk me into the waiting ambulance, having responded to the emergency call. Things would happen so fast. I pictured my mother, forlorn, fighting to be with me but they would not let her, so urgent was my situation. Almost overwhelmed by my own mental picture, I rushed to find my mom, and in an urgent voice I told her I needed an immediate audience with her. She left what she was doing and took me to her room. In its privacy, between choking sobs I pleaded my innocence. "Mommy," I cried, "I didn't do anything—honest." Somehow I managed to blurt out a disjointed story explaining the calamity that had befallen me. As I finished my tale, pleading my innocence, I awaited her verdict with bated breath.

Her calm response, accompanied with a kind, knowing smile, threw me off balance completely. In fact, I was sorely disappointed, and slight indignation welled up in me as she nodded understandingly and proceeded to initiate me into the use of a sanitary napkin. Thereafter she guided me through the fundamentals of the new phase of life I had unwittingly come into. Somberly she explained to me that I had crossed the threshold from girlhood to womanhood. This sounded like serious business. I learned in mother's lecture that gone forever was my "childhood." This was good stuff, better than a library membership! A surge of pride darted through me. Yet it was with mixed feelings I was to say adieu to tomboy frolics in exchange for this crossing. More unsettling was the feeling I had as I listened and realized that I was going to be denied full liberty of myself for approximately one week each month. This was the price I had to pay for the honor of ascending to womanhood.

This event ushered in the crossroads of puberty, a growing-up period I understood poorly. The bridge between the ugly duckling and the graceful swan was difficult for me to cross, and I floundered for the too long a time it took to make the traverse. I seethed in resentment at not being more padded in obvious areas of my femininity. Daily I struggled with exercises to increase the upper part of my torso in a ritual chant of "I must, I must, I must increase my bust!" I tried to inject a swagger in my walk to prove that I had come of age—as I saw grown women do. (I was, after all, now a woman.) I groped the air wildly in a bid to understand a stage of growing up where no one proffered me any suggestions.

When I was about thirteen years of age, and practically every girl in my class required the added assistance of a brassiere, I took out some pocket money and bought myself a size 29A bra. I bent over severally to pick up an imaginary object. The whole performance had the singular aim of drawing attention to me. I wanted my classmates to become aware of the fact that I had graduated from flat chest level to well…a bra-needing and wearing level. The plan was for the strap outlines of my bra to show against the uniform fabric when bent over. At last this unusual clumsiness caught on, and someone finally got smart! Everyone's attention was called to the fact that I was now a proud wearer of a brassiere. Rather than blush at this brash publicity, I was emboldened and actually gratified in its crudity. This identification rite, I believed, was the final service I needed to make me on par with my colleagues. It was the conclusive finish to being recognized and respectfully accepted in the community of my peers.

Time passed. Days turned to months and months trickled to years, and I still remained a size 29A user. Somehow I got the impression that being a bra-user would actually stimulate a speedier chest development, but to my utter dismay, it appeared that I had stagnated. I pored over this stunted growth with resentment and savagely turned in on myself. I took on a brutal deprecatory stance aimed at me, and in twisted, satirical humor, I mocked myself and ridiculed my physique. I became my own tormentor and donned an external protective clad of uncomplimentary self-labels: "figure 1," "letter I," and so on. When I wanted to be nice to me, I assumed my build was "athletic." I was hard on me to shield me from the possible pain of another's hurtful words. I reasoned that if I looked the part, I might as well dress accordingly. I was convinced that my back view offered no different view than that of a boy, so I maintained a wardrobe consistent with my belief: T-shirts, jeans, and sneakers. Those were years when I was engulfed by a dire sense of low self-esteem.

Today, too many girls and women suffer an extremely disjointed and unbalanced view of themselves, which greatly affects their attitude and self-confidence. Profligate images taunt the concept of femalehood and assault the eyes at every turn on billboards and magazine covers, communicating in strong terms a language of body worship. The female's attraction is projected as external, being a summation of body curves all over. As the body form is thus vaunted, character values are ignored. Unwary, little, innocent girls have their tender minds primed to respond and indeed to desire the lewd. The assault is more subtle, and the sensual creeps into homes in the form of voluptuous dolls and animated heroine characters, which effectively awaken and mold a little girl's thinking to a more definite interest in her physical appearance and nurtures an inner secret wish to be more like her doll or her favorite TV figure.

The true jewel of a woman's beauty resides not on the outside but on the inside. Work on releasing your inner beauty. Work on making the crossing.

Crossing…

...passing from one phase to another as the beauty of your person emerges in growth.

Crossing...

...the traverse from girlhood to womanhood emotionally, physically, and spiritually.

Crossing...

...the departure from childish play and the entry into studied maturity.

Crossing...

...the switch from tomboy slouching to a delicate ladylike poise.

Crossing...

...the acceptance and attendant care that follows the distinct evolvements of femininity in the physiology.

Crossing...

...the nostalgia of bidding farewell to boyish habits and welcoming the erudite vesture of ladyship.

Crossing...

...the joy of a new unfolding world, born in a new unfolding body.

Crossing...

...the freshness of beauty in blossom.

Crossing.

Chapter six

Celebrating Life

JESUS IS THE center. All life evolves from Him and must revolve around Him to be truly meaningful. Every day reveals varying nuances of thought in regard to our mortality and eternity. Truth,[6] however, though it passes through the storms of ambiguity and disagreement, remains unchangingly the same and is the only guarantee of salvation.[7] In spite of all arguments based on human rationalization, the infallible Word of God stands immovable against the sands of time. Forms of religion, in sects and cults, advance misinformation in their professions of "ways" to reach God in fellowship.[8] Were it not so tragic in the eternal peril, it would have been amusing in noting that though a majority of religions acknowledge in some subtle way the person of Jesus Christ, they clearly deny His Lordship and sovereignty. He is accorded a meaningless position or level in the framework of these forms of spiritual falsehood.[9] This act of deliberate denial is mischievous, as will be seen someday when all mankind confesses (willingly or

---

6 "And ye shall know the truth, and the truth shall make you free" (John 8:32).

7 "For this is good and acceptable in the sight of God our Saviour; who will have all men to be saved, and to come unto the knowledge of the truth. For there is one God, and one mediator between God and men, the man Christ Jesus" (1 Timothy 2:3–5).

8 "There is a way which seemeth right unto a man, but the end thereof are the ways of death" (Proverbs 14:12).

9 "Professing themselves to be wise, they became fools, and changed the glory of the uncorruptible God into an image made like to corruptible man" (Romans 1:22–23).

unwillingly) the Lordship of Jesus.[10] The Scriptures are explicit in the one only acceptable intermediary between man and God—the man, Christ Jesus.[11]

Indeed, too often when eternity is brought before a person in the choice of a life-and-death decision in accepting or rejecting Jesus Christ as Savior, the individual's reasoning seems dulled. This exhilarating, life-promising invitation actually sparks an internal struggle. How many persons would give a second thought consideration at life in the event of an impending plane crash? There would be a pandemonium and struggle to reach the exit or whatever means of escape were available! Why? Because people want to live. So much energy is expended in insuring what is but a fragment of our time here on earth, when ironically the clock of eternity ticks on. With every turned-down salvation offer, a person is brought closer to the final death stamp and seal of everlasting perdition. You make the difference in your choice—to partake in the life now and everlasting, or to walk the path of death now and obtain a ticket to an unending damnation. The free flow of Jesus's love is available to you today in order that you may begin a definite celebration of life.

You see, the mystery of life lies in the blood. The shedding of the blood and the final death of Jesus Christ was a dramatic event of proxy. He took upon Himself the death that we were all deserving. Hanging on that cross, His sinless blood flowed out as the ultimate expression of His love for mankind. A divine exchange ensued when His blood was poured out for us. For that pouring out represented the washing, the cleansing, and the atonement that blots out all our sinfulness.[12] Everyone who would acknowledge this supreme

---

[10] "That at the name of Jesus every knee should bow, of things in heaven and things in earth, and things under the earth; and that every tongue should confess that Jesus Christ is Lord, to the glory of God the Father" (Philippians 2:10–11).

[11] "For there is one God, and one mediator between God and men, the man Christ Jesus" (1 Timothy 2:5).

[12] "But Christ being come as high priest of good things to come…by his own blood he entered in once into the holy place, having obtained

sacrifice and take advantage of the gift of life would also enjoy the glorious covenant promises hid in the gift. It is an error of judgment to think that forms of penance such as self-flagellation or a multitude of virtuous acts of charity will someday make us acceptable before God. We are saved not by works but by grace. God makes it clear that outside His way[13] (Jesus) and terms[14] (Jesus), every humanitarian act of philanthropy remains nothing more than that—a humanitarian act and not a divine act.[15] The divine act is rested in Jesus. This is the act that is embedded in recreative power.

The pain of labor attempts to becloud the beauty of life in birth, but birth bursts forth and joy is released in an avalanche of rejoicing. So far you may have walked in circles and resisted God's gift. The time is now to make your life-giving decision. Life is in the blood. Cease the struggle today, and enter into God's covenant plenty through the priceless blood of Jesus Christ.

Life is in the blood. Menstruation is the symbolic link to life, in that blood is shed. It is a divinely charted calendar within which rests the promise of continuity in birth. This blood sign is the affirmation that a girl is capable of birthing life. Outside menstruation, new life cannot be hosted. God has bestowed this singular honor and esteem upon the female Adam.

---

eternal redemption for us.... And almost all things are by the law purged with blood; and without shedding of blood is no remission....And as it is appointed unto men once to die, but after this the judgment: So Christ was once offered to bear the sins of many....For it is not possible that the blood of bulls and of goats should take away sins" (Hebrews 9:11–12, 22, 27–28; 10:4).
13 "Jesus saith...I am the way, the truth, and the life: no man cometh unto the Father, but by me" (John 14:6).
14 "There is a way which seemeth right unto a man, but the end thereof are the ways of death" (Proverbs 14:12).
15 "But we are all as an unclean thing, and all our righteousness are as filthy rags; and we all do fade as a leaf; and our iniquities, like the wind, have taken us away" (Isaiah 64:6).

The menstrual cycle is the cycle of changes in the female human reproductive organs. It culminates in uterine bleeding about every twenty-eight days when the ovum (egg) is not fertilized by a male sperm. It is significant to note that in menstruation, the womb is being prepared for pregnancy. The mucous lining of the womb is set in readiness to host the fetus. However, when a fetus is not forthcoming, the mucous lining is discharged in the form of menses, which comes out as blood. This shedding of blood is a constant reminder that new life can be birthed.

The womb is the unborn baby's (or babies') abode for the gestation period of nine months. The womb is the female activity center responsible for the changes that every young girl will undergo. The ovaries are the two female reproductive organs within the womb that produce eggs and female sex hormones (estrogen). These hormones are responsible for the production of female sexual characteristics such as the growth of breasts, shapes of hips, tone of voice, and, ultimately, the maintenance of the process of the menstrual cycle.

This vital stage of growth is one that a young girl should enter into with warm welcome. Its advent is the herald of forthcoming blessings in the bringing forth, nurture, and sustenance of humanity's cords.

Flower assumes a stubborn indifference to her situation. It is barely twelve weeks since she put a stop to the pill popping, and she is resolved to live her life normally. Her ears are deaf to voices of concern as well as criticism, and in this unpreoccupied state of mind, she is puttering about the plants in the garden. Flower feels something. She shrugs off the feeling as the cold weather's tease. It is not unnatural on a cold day for the chill to play on her body this way, causing a slight increase in a natural, normal female discharge. However, after a little while, she begins to feel uneasy, a little

Celebrating Life

heavy. Quietly she goes indoors and retreats to her bathroom. On checking herself, she is suffused with a mix of overwhelming relief and joy. At last! The dam has burst and the flow is on! What a moment for Flower, what joy unspeakable! But speak she must, and the news is announced to mother, whose shrieks of gladness bring father rushing into the room. Once in the picture, it's his turn to bounce on springs of joy!

The home is hit with heaves of hilarity and rocked agog with much jocundity! Breathless activity scuttles to and fro! A name list is prepared, invitation cards are distributed!

The festive air hangs thick and is heightened with father calling in a band! A feast is spread and punch flows! What is the occasion for the pomp and fanfare? What is the cause for this showy, colorful effervescence? What could be the reason for such merriment? Proclaim it loud for all to hear! This overflowing joyful exhibition has at its center, Flower's ascent to womanhood! Roll the drums and declare abroad; this is a celebration of life!

If you meet Flower on the streets, you will recognize her instantly. She is that young woman with a sprint in her step, an infectious laugh, a studied speech, a penchant look, and an indomitable spirit—a conveyor of confidence! She is that young woman, well mannered, respectful, and discriminatory in her eating habits, a core of correct attitudes, displaying a delightful demeanor at all times. The magnetism of her attraction lies in her naturalness. She vibrates life and an energy directly drawn from her Maker.

You will recognize Flower if you meet her on the streets. She is the young woman who walks with the bursting pride of being a privileged monthly cycle beneficiary.

Part III

Bloom

Let no man despise thy youth; but be thou an example of the believers, in word, in conversation, in charity, in spirit, in faith, in purity.

1 Timothy 4:12

Chapter seven

Petals

THE BUD BLOSSOMS and the petals explode in full bloom. The girl budded has blossomed into a maiden, and her full bloom has come in womanhood.

All the petals of her outward person converge in an inner identification. The physical attributes of height, weight, complexion, and more add up to her outer person, the seen person. Yet of more poignancy is the color of the petals as fed from within the plant.

Colors varied pour forth in expressions of temperament and personality. Bright colors shimmer laughingly while somber colors, subdued in reflective tones, whisper quietly; pastel colors, gentle and passive, smile delicately while blended colors of indefinite nuance and hues dance sprightly to life's tune. The petals' colors, singular and particular, similar but distinctly different, offer a vivid, unmatchable uniqueness, marking the individual's peculiar personality blend.

Color is an attribute of things that result from the light they reflect.

God declares that you are His workmanship![16] Workmanship speaks of the skillfulness required of an artisan. You did not fall off the production line from a mass production center. The Master Artist deployed His imagination and creative skills on you, concentrating exclusively in designing and forming you! Though one of twins, triplets, quadruplets, quints, or more, identical though you

---

16 "For we are His workmanship, created in Christ Jesus unto good works, which God hath before ordained that we should walk in them" (Ephesians 2:10).

may be with one or more siblings, each of you is singularly different, fashioned one at a time by God the Creator. Do you doubt this? Science proves it in the individual preserve of each person's fingerprint and also in each person's peculiar DNA structure. Woman, you are beautiful! You are delicately molded, carefully sculpted, and lovingly touched with strokes of gentleness from the Master's brush. From conception God deftly formed you with painstaking affection.

Color is an attribute of things that result from the light they reflect. It is only in Christ Jesus that you can shine brightest as He causes you to flourish in good works. What light do you reflect?[17]

The more you reflect God's light, the richer your color quotient. The less you reflect God's light, the more apparent is your lack of depth of color. Is your life's color vivid or faded? Distinct or decrepit? Authentic or counterfeit? Look inward into yourself.

Are your colors graced with the velvet softness of kindness and laced with a pattern of longsuffering meshed with faith? Are your colors audacious in expressions of joy, bold in strong stolid strokes of faith? Are the colors of your action reflective of the light and love of Christ?

Many plants have earned their names through their display of lush and rich colors. Of proof are the mauve and bluish hues of the violet…the yellow or orange flowers in the marigold…the ice plant combination of leaves with ice-like hairs and pinkish white rayed flowers. What name have the colors of your actions earned you? Gracious, gentle, generous? Or unpleasant, unkind, or…too debasing to mention?

The petals' colors are a source of influence, determining the plant kind, playing a central role in character dominance. Splayed colors offer a different theme: attractive, depressive, spell-binding, confusing, transparent, secretive, disquieting, or relaxing. Your actions are ultimately linked to your person. Do you attract or repel?

---

[17] "Ye are the light of the world.…Let your light so shine before men, that they may see your good works, and glorify your Father which is in heaven"(Matthew 5:14, 16).

Petals

The petals of your personality speak of your upbringing and background. They speak of your values and your character worth. What do you do in the face of temptation when compromise's allure beckons at you?

Flower is at a defining moment in her relationship with long-time friends. She has incurred the wrath of friends she grew up with by her firm stance not to follow the crowd. They hurl hurtful words at her and attempt to diminish the nobility of her choice because it does not conform with theirs. They insinuate that she is "not with it," is a "sissy" and "a prude putting up a holier-than-thou act." In derision they nickname her "prissy prude." She is hurt deeply by these cutting terms. Nonetheless, she remains firm in her decision, established by her unwavering conviction. Flower is resolute to remain chaste, having solemnly vowed to God that she would honor Him by maintaining the sanctity of her body—a holy temple.[18]

A little voice within chides her that she really is being a mite too fussy. After all, it isn't as if she has been invited to an orgy! It's just a group date, Flower! I mean, how safe can you get? In a group date you each look out for the other. Or should. The nagging, unsettling feeling she senses within is a knowing feeling—an internal alarm that rings a warning—cautioning her to stand her guard and watch out from making an emotionally unwise decision.

She hears the seething voice of an angry and irritable friend: "You are just too inflexible!" She fights back the tear threatening to pop over her lids and slide down her cheek. She finds herself almost nodding in silent agreement. Then her closest friend derides her, with a look so intense in disdain and disgust that Flower physically catches her breath. Sarcastically she summarizes the situation and says in a curt voice, "Flower is betrothed to Jesus. He'll be putting a

---

18 "Know ye not that your body is the temple of the Holy Ghost which is in you, which ye have of God, and ye are not your own?" (1 Corinthians 6:19).

wedding ring on her finger. You know, she's sold out to Him being her groom and she being the bride." The raucous laughter from all was a nail in *her* cross. She flinched but kept a brave face. The words, though spoken unkindly, testified rightly. When she spoke, her voice conveyed an emotional steel that surprised even her. "I am just one," she said. "I don't see how my personal decision affects you to the extent that you exhibit such animosity. You do what you think is good for you. I am doing what I know is best for me. Single, double, blind, or any other type of date is not for me. I'll go dating only when I am prepared for the responsibility of marriage—which isn't right now." There was quiet. As often is the case when one person stands out on principles of integrity, Flower was the thorn in their flesh. In her stance she exposed the doubtfulness of their motives.

Picking up her bag, she rose from the table. A sad smile tipped her lips. "Bye, girls," she said gently, sadly. The air hung thick and quiet.

Turning her back on them, a restrained tear finding its way down her cheeks, she walked away. Her insides churned and she hurt very badly, as though she had been struck a physical blow in her stomach. These were her friends. They had done so much together. The laughter, the fun, the fears, the challenges…they had gone it together. But now? For a bunch of boys of doubtful origins, granted, very handsome, they had thrown her out and were going to throw caution to the wind? She argued with herself. There is safety in numbers. What a lame case that made. "Do not be unequally yoked with unbelievers," came the Scripture word to her. She sighed. The number theory waned to nothingness in the face of the unsound mix. She wanted to cast a fleeting glance back but stopped herself. There was nothing she could do, she concluded, but one. She whispered a prayer, "Lord, show them mercy, and please keep them from all evil."

Walking on, she concluded that she would go home and enjoy a home date with her folks.

Chapter eight

Fragrance

From within a woman wells up a spring. It could be of a delicate fragrance or an insupportable stench. If the former, it is translated in a flow of appeal; if the latter, it is a repellant. The beautiful fragrance is the one that is overwhelming in adornments of graciousness and decorum, in behavior as in speech.

Fragrance is perceived in words…

Fragrance: …soft, thoughtful, seasoned with salt; kind and encouraging, wholesome and pure. Backbiting, malice, curt remarks cutting—poisons venomous, evils to flee.

Fragrance: …particular and perennial, gracious and respectful. "Thank you," "Please," "I am sorry"; these are keys to open the most unwilling doors. Commands and orders avoid completely.

Fragrance: …spoken in tones pleasurable. Welcome the strokes soothing, kind and gentle. Away the abrasive and corrosive, qualities harsh, raspy, nagging off putting—such to the user's loss.

Fragrance is perceived in an act;

Fragrance: …dripping with love, concern, and care. In warmth of kindness, pleasing, and rewarding.

Fragrance: …modest, unpretentious, sacrificial in help. For the sake of another's comfort, denying oneself.

Fragrance: …industrious, determined, persevering, and unrelenting, even in the face of the most assiduous tasks.

Fragrance is perceived in the attitude;

Fragrance: …benevolent, meek, open-hearted and ready, willing to be corrected.

Fragrance: ...wholesome and healthy, seeing the good in every situation.

Fragrance: ...understanding, forgiving, holding no grudge against any.

Determine your fragrance today. You hold the power and sway to emit a beautiful fragrance.

Beauty is the utterance from within your heart formed in speech. Time will command the manner of speech used, and the manner of speech used will command the time. Self-control in speech is a strong determiner of the future. Know that the times will allow occasion for a soft word to apply balm to a hurt; a firm word to maintain order; and no word spoken in the quiet language of wisdom.

Beauty is the accommodating aspect of behavior, the unspoken utterance of speech acted.

The fragrance of beauty is sweet and desirous. The desire to be beautiful is an inborn, God-given, God-planted sensibility resident in every woman. A woman should work at cultivating both beauties: the inner beauty in depth of character substance and the external beauty in terms of caring for the body. A beautiful woman is complete in the dual attributes.

The seed of beauty starts with self-acceptance. Appreciate your wholesomeness in God. When you look into the mirror, recognize with humble thanks that you are His design, the product of His artistry and the result of His love. You are the crown of God's creative masterpiece!

Flower's perfume exudes a sweetness such to intoxicate the senses; it invades the air in unseen essence and permeates the atmosphere in an invisible yet tangible presence.

Fragrance

I recall a woman whose fragrance thoroughly invaded my senses.

I was about ten years of age when I was introduced to my girlfriend's parents. Even at that age, my immediate thought on meeting the couple was that they were an evident mismatch. The physical handsomeness of the man stood in sharp contrast to the physical blandness of his wife. I went through the formalities and politeness of exchanging greetings and answering small talk.

As I waited for my friend, I scrutinized this woman and thought my friend fortunate not to be a spitting image of her mother. My bias formed thicker as I studied her, sympathized with her dressing, no, the dress was OK, it was her shape that blunted the beauty of the attire. Maybe the custom in this part of the world was for a woman to bring a handsome dowry and thereby attract eligible suitors? Where I come from, men pay a dowry for the bride. My thoughts kept adrift. Unexplainably, at what precise moment I cannot tell, I found myself enjoying the company of my friend's mother. A rich warmth had captured the atmosphere, and her charm filled the air. There was an unfeigned naturalness of love and kindness about her person, and it provided a trusting berth to moor in. Suddenly, with doused shock, I realized that all my former bias had melted away. Unconsciously I began to study her afresh. She still was as before. What was I expecting? A physical transformation? There was none. The unglamorous exterior was intact and well.

Then it dawned upon me. A simple but most valuable lesson took a seat in my soul: true beauty is not skin deep but heart deep.

Chapter nine

The Flower

FLOWER IS PARTICULARLY careful in her toilette today. She has taken her bath and reaches out for the deodorant stick, which she applies to her armpits. Today she cannot afford the slightest whiff from perspiration. Today is much too special!

Standing at decision junction, she is at a loss at what to wear! A white straight dress is pulled off the hanger, but almost immediately she decides against it. To successfully wear white against her rich brown skin would require that she uses dark underwear. Not ready to go through all the trouble of redressing from scratch, she considers the alternatives. She disqualifies as too playful the bright, flowery prints that beckon at her. This is not a picnic, she chides herself. But she must hurry; oh, why had she not sorted this bit out the night before? A sultry black dress with a mid-waist accompanying jacket brings a little hesitation. In the hot afternoon sun, which would come in the next couple of hours, she would absolutely melt under its relentless rays. Besides, that dress was more suitable for an evening occasion. Finally she decides on a navy blue trouser suit that speaks a language of correctness in a blend of friendly seriousness. She contrasts this evenly with a simple white blouse.

Looking herself over in the mirror, Flower nods approval. She combs through her mane of hair and relishes the free bounce of the light bob she wears.

A quick glance at the clock tells her she'll have to live with the slightly chipped polish on her little finger. No time for a touch up. Flower's makeup is in tune with her mood—light and easy. She finishes her toilette in a 'Must' de Cartier signature perfume; in an instant the fragrance permeates the room. She tosses the bottle into her functional leather handbag. Standing tall to her full six-foot height, Flower looks herself over in the mirror and nods a final approval at her reflection. Her squeaky clean, well-polished, sturdy, all-purpose shoes smile back at her in their black shine. She slings her bag on her shoulder and steps out, ready for her first job interview!

Flower has grown from that moment when she made her entry into the world with a cry that brought forth rejoicing from her parents and well-wishers alike. She has evolved into a very sensitive, caring, and responsible young woman. Her sense of responsibility is portrayed more sharply in situations not too pleasant, as in the case of the dating issue. Such a situation forces her to make a stance based on the prevailing knowledge she has of right and wrong and the correct application of this knowledge. This is wisdom, and wisdom is the essence of the mature person. Flower does not rely on her feelings, which she has come to understand to be as fickle as they are fleeting. Neither does she vaunt herself in a pretentious sense of self-reliance, but she seeks wisdom's recourse in making the right decision at the right moment, each time, every time.

Looking good is a sound choice. When you look good, you feel good and you act likewise. The flip side of the coin reveals a reverse pattern. Look lousy, feel lousy—and your chances are much increased to act accordingly.

However, the ability to major on the external does not guarantee the perfection of the internal workings. A person is as he thinks, and he confirms his substance in the reflection of his behavior.

Maturity is...

...the recognition and acceptance of responsibilities.

...a balanced response to issues and not a weighted argument.

The Flower

...confronting crisis with perfect mind stability and not irascible spontaneity.

...maintaining the equilibrium of normalcy in the face of stifling pressures.

Maturity should not be confounded with age, for it is not a given of years accrued.

Too many adults indulge themselves in outbursts of cantankerous anger. They release billows of vexation through pounding and kicking furniture and bellow out brutish orders. These are merely adults in age but in reasoning remain mental juveniles. Apologetically, such persons are given to pettiness, sullen jealousy, and bitter envy. They are easily ticked off and are quick to engage themselves in a comparison flout. Undeniably, such adults are captives of a spoiled childhood; they remain subdued to the dominance of indulgences they never learned to control. They are the products of a laissez-faire youth; now they have become the retch of adulthood.

They are immature.

Perhaps you are pressed in on every side by the sweltering pressures of life. How much easier to recoil inward and wish these pressures away...but you know that they won't just go that way. If you can but view the pain and distress of now, though real and poignant, as a refining passage leading on to the glorious end of a winding road where the freshness of a new beginning commences, you will find the necessary strength to forge ahead.

We stand responsible for our decisions, our judgments. We further stand responsible for the consequences of our judgments. It is imprudent to point blame at another and say, "He made me do it." No person is powerful enough to cause you to act in a particular way, unless you turn the reins of power over your life to another. If this be the case, it is time to take back your life! Choice is man's gift to exercise at will; don't lose it!

Today, make the decision to stand accountable for you. Excise childish ways and rule.[19]

I can do nothing about my past. The present is full, but the future is laced with potential. I learn from my past and I move on to my tomorrow by investing in my today.

I have said words I ought not to have. I have acted in ways I shouldn't have. I have made costly mistakes, lost opportunities, and done things wrongly. But I view them all as advantages—wisdom's nuggets, precious learning points. Experiences framed to bless another, guide another, caution another.

I can do nothing about my past. The present is full, and the future is laced with potential.

I must move on.

---

19 "When I was a child, I spake as a child, I understood as a child, I thought as a child: but when I became a man, I put away childish things" (1 Corinthians 13:11).

Epilogue

When Eve ate the forbidden fruit and offered some of the same to her husband, Adam, the Bible records that their eyes were opened. The next line of action for these two disobedient adult children proved very interesting and most revealing. First, they sewed leaves together and made themselves aprons. Second, they hid themselves from the presence of the Lord God. When God came in His customary manner in the cool of the evening to enjoy their company, Adam was nowhere to be found. God called out to Adam, and the besmitten fellow quaked and his shaky reply was, "I was afraid because I was naked; and I hid myself" (Gen. 3:10).

In this statement is the explanation behind the first Scripture recorded game of hide and seek. Hide and seek is a universally accepted game that has attained global popularity among children and unparalleled levels with the adult population.

The more seasoned in age perfect the game by the moment and play it with sophisticated dexterity and technological triumph, discovering more intricate hideouts camouflaged in creative exteriors. The female Adam shows greater ingenuity in the game. She cloaks herself in pretentious airs, wraps her insecurities in volumes of makeup, and desperately seeks to affirm her person through an unrelenting drive in purpose that tends to the mercenary. She constantly seeks fresh burrows in which to hide, curled up within herself in the lavish void of emptiness. The fresh aprons she wears continue to prove inadequate, and her frustration mounts. There will be no end to this game until she turns to God, through Jesus Christ, to be filled with the incomprehensible richness of His love.

Only then will her frailties be turned to strengths, her insecurities melted forever, her person find true fulfillment.

Dear friend, you have to accept that each covering you wear is both temporary and unsatisfactory. Too quickly discontent sets in anew, and like a ball on the roulette wheel, the cycle continues as the ball spins around and around and around…until it comes to rest—not as planned, but by chance—anywhere. God did not create you to lead an anyhow life that ends anywhere. Indeed you are too precious to be gambled, and this is why Jesus died and rose again to give your life true meaning in His love.

Though you've tried hard, you must admit that the makeup doesn't cover it, the chic clothing can't conceal it, and the change in career status won't seal it. This sad note has been the refrain too long played in your life. Change is now come to your doorstep, waiting upon you to make the decision.

The more layers of outer coverings, the deeper the depth of your hiding place within the recesses of yourself. Though you are adrift and feeling so far from God, He is waiting for you lovingly and patiently.

It's time to return to the time when *bliss* and *peace* were the live-in words for the male and female Adam. Don't waste a moment longer of the valuable time you don't have to keep. As long as the gift of breath remains in you, in applause to life and as a tribute to womanhood, carry yourself with dignity!

Relax and take in a deep breath. Tell God, "Father, I turn my life over to You through Your Son, Jesus. Help me to understand who I am in You, Lord Jesus, that I might really begin to live life as You always meant for me to live it—meaningfully. I love You, Lord. Thank You! In Jesus's name, Amen."

Step out, sister, and fill those lungs with life—His life! Don't stop at being God's creation; you are the crown of His creation!

You are yesterday's bud, blossoming out today in readiness to become tomorrow's full bloom!

I love you.

About the Author

TANI O. IFEDIORA was born in Lagos, Nigeria on August 4, 1963. Her global cross-cultural appreciation is due to a variegated educational background, derived from an early exposure to schooling in Belgium, France, Botswana, and Nigeria. In 1984 she obtained a Bachelor of Arts degree in French from the University of Nigeria, Nsukka. Presently, Tani heads a Human Resource Consultancy, Courtoisie Character Refiners Limited, which accents personal enhancement, social graces, and leadership grooming. She is frequently invited to speak at various concerns: business, non-profit, women, and youth groups. Tani is happily married to Chukie Ifediora, and together they are blessed with three sons and two daughters.

Contact the Author

WEBSITE:
WWW.COURTOISIENG.COM
TELEPHONE:
+234 8023131849

www.ingramcontent.com/pod-product-compliance
Lightning Source LLC
Chambersburg PA
CBHW071410040426
42444CB00009B/2183